Salary Figures

A Codebook of Expectations

Dmitry Vostokov

Published by OpenTask, Republic of Ireland

OpenTask codebooks are available through booksellers and distributors worldwide. For further information or comments send requests to press@opentask.com.

ISBN-13: 978-1-906717-46-9 (Paperback)

First printing, 2009

1,000

2,000

3,000

4,000

5,000

6,000

7,000

8,000

9,000

10,000

15,000

20,000

25,000

30,000

35,000

40,000

45,000

50,000

55,000

60,000

65,000

70,000

75,000

80,000

85,000

90,000

95,000

100,000

105,000

110,000

115,000

120,000

125,000

130,000

135,000

140,000

145,000

150,000

155,000

160,000

165,000

170,000

175,000

180,000

185,000

190,000

195,000

200,000

210,000

220,000

230,000

240,000

250,000

260,000

270,000

280,000

290,000

300,000

310,000

320,000

330,000

340,000

350,000

360,000

370,000

380,000

390,000

400,000

410,000

420,000

430,000

440,000

450,000

460,000

470,000

480,000

490,000

500,000

550,000

600,000

650,000

700,000

750,000

800,000

850,000

900,000

950,000

1,000,000

Perks

Stock options

Company car

Pension

Life

insurance

Bonus

Medical insurance

Educational

assistance

Gym

Relocation

package